P9-BZT-706

Avon, Mass. 02322

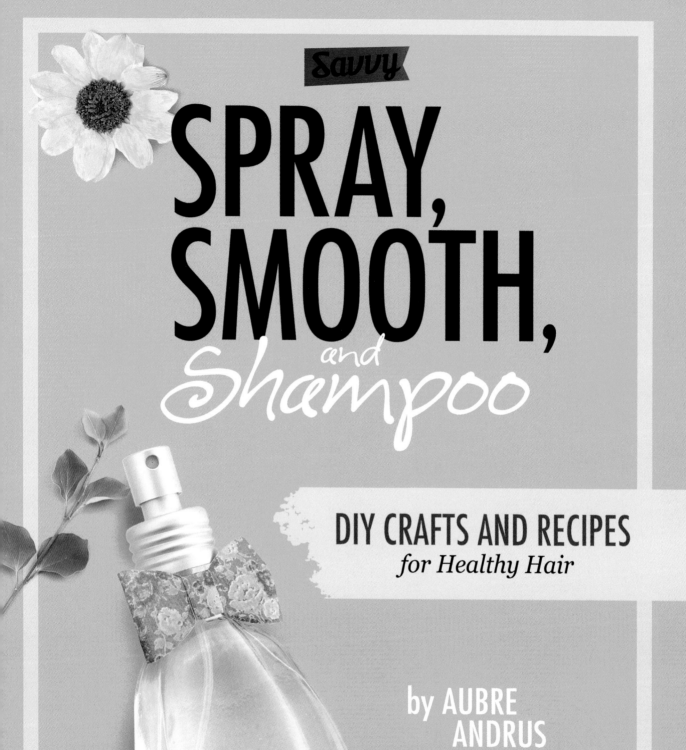

Savvy

SPRAY, SMOOTH, *and Shampoo*

DIY CRAFTS AND RECIPES
for Healthy Hair

by AUBRE ANDRUS

CAPSTONE PRESS
a capstone imprint

Savvy Books are published by Capstone Press,
1710 Roe Crest Drive, North Mankato, Minnesota 56003
www.mycapstone.com

Library of Congress Cataloging-in-Publication Data
Names: Andrus, Aubre, author.
Title: Spray, smooth, and shampoo : DIY crafts and recipes for healthy hair
by Aubre Andrus.
Description: North Mankato, Minnesota : Capstone Press, [2017] | Series:
Savvy. DIY Day Spa | Audience: Age 9-13. | Audience: Grade 4 to 6. |
Identifiers: LCCN 2016030038| ISBN 9781515734444 (library binding) |
ISBN 9781515734482 (eBook PDF)
Subjects: LCSH: Hair—Care and hygiene—Juvenile literature. |
Handicraft—Juvenile literature.
Classification: LCC RL91 .A53 2017 | DDC 646.7/24—dc23
LC record available at https://lccn.loc.gov/2016030038

Editor: Eliza Leahy
Designer: Tracy McCabe
Creative Director: Heather Kindseth
Production Specialist: Katy LaVigne

Image Credits: Photographs by Capstone Studio: Karon Dubke,
photographer; Sarah Schuette, photo stylist; Marcy Morin,
studio scheduler; Author photo by Ariel Andrus

Printed and bound in the USA.
010062S17

TABLE OF CONTENTS

INTRODUCTION

Creating a spa experience at home is easier than you might think. Believe it or not, you'll find a lot of what you need in the kitchen!

The recipes in this book aren't much different from traditional recipes (such as cupcakes, cookies, and cake), but these recipes aren't meant to be eaten. Instead of soothing your hunger, these recipes will nourish your hair. We'll take on tangles, frizz, and dull hair with everything from dry shampoos to sprays to gels to masks.

But we won't stop there. In addition to the hair care, we will give your hair some flair! You'll need to make a trip to the craft store because you won't want to miss out on the do-it-yourself projects for headbands, decorative pins, and more.

Start flipping through this book until a project catches your eye. There's no wrong or right place to start. Enjoy these spa products alone, give them as gifts, or invite some friends over for a party.

IT'S TIME TO PAMPER YOURSELF!

SPECIALTY INGREDIENTS

Some of the recipes in this book call for simple ingredients that you may already have in your kitchen, such as baking soda or olive oil. But there are some specialty ingredients that you likely won't find at home.

Luckily, they can be found at health food stores or organic grocery stores near the spices, pharmacy, or beauty aisles. You can also find them online. Here are some of those ingredients and the reasons you need them in your recipes.

aloe vera gel

shea butter

cocoa powder

Aloe Vera Gel – *Aloe vera gel moisturizes skin and hair, as well as soothes thanks to the cooling effect.*

Cocoa Powder – *This chocolate powder can be found in the baking aisle of grocery stores. It is used as a natural, temporary hair dye.*

Coconut Oil – *Coconut oil moisturizes your skin and hair.*

Distilled Water – *Distilled water has been boiled to remove impurities, and it will help your ingredients last longer. It can be found at grocery stores.*

Jojoba Oil – *Jojoba oil is soothing when applied to skin and can help condition damaged hair.*

Rosewater – *Rosewater soothes and strengthens skin, and it conditions hair too. It has a floral perfume-like aroma.*

Sea Salt – *Sea salt can help form soft waves in your hair, making it look like you just went for a swim in the ocean.*

Shea Butter – *Shea butter moisturizes and conditions hair.*

Vegetable Glycerin – *Vegetable glycerin naturally attracts moisture and can help smooth unruly hair.*

ESSENTIAL OILS

Many of the recipes in this book call for essential oils. Essential oils are used for aromatherapy (they smell lovely and can make you feel great) and for health benefits for your hair, skin, and body.

They can be found at health food stores, organic grocery stores, or online. Here are the essential oils used in this book and the reasons you might use them in your recipes.

Lavender

Lavender is probably the most popular essential oil. It can soothe skin and possibly help fight acne. It has a floral aroma that can help you fall asleep.

Roman Chamomile

Roman chamomile essential oil soothes skin and has a calming aroma that can help you wind down and clear your sinuses.

Orange*

Orange essential oil is a natural cleanser and deodorizer, and it can help heal skin. Its citrus aroma is energizing.

Peppermint

Peppermint essential oil has a cooling effect. It can relieve muscle pain and has an invigorating aroma that can make you feel alert.

Be careful! Don't allow any undiluted essential oil to get on your skin or in your eyes or mouth. Recipes from this book containing essential oils should not be used on children under age 6, and for older children, an adult's help is recommended.

*Orange essential oil could be phototoxic, which means it can make your skin extra-sensitive to the sun. Don't apply to bare skin before going outside. And always wear sunscreen!

MEASURING YOUR INGREDIENTS

Essential oils are very potent and must be diluted with distilled water or a carrier oil, such as coconut oil, jojoba oil, or olive oil. It might not seem like you're using a lot, but a little goes a long way!

The recipes in this book dilute the essential oil to about 1 percent. That means some recipes require only a few drops. We measure essential oils by the drop in this book because it's hard to measure any other way. (There are 20 drops in 1 milliliter, and ¼ teaspoon is a little more than 1 milliliter.) There are very few recipes that will require more than ¼ teaspoon of essential oil.

coconut oil

jojoba oil

olive oil

HOW TO SAFELY MELT BUTTER AND OIL

Shea butter is a soft solid that must be melted. A double boiler is best for melting oils and butters, but you can also microwave them at 50 percent power in 30-second increments, stirring in between, until the solid is almost all the way melted. Stir to complete the melting process. You don't want to overheat the oils or butters.

Coconut oil is also used in this book. Whether your coconut oil is a solid or a liquid depends on where you live, what time of year it is, and the air temperature. To solidify it, place it in the refrigerator until it hardens. To liquefy it, heat it in a microwave-safe bowl in 10-second increments at 50 percent power, stirring in between, until the solid is almost all the way melted.

It's best to heat the solids in a microwave-safe bowl with a pourable spout and a handle, such as a glass Pyrex measuring cup. Be sure to always wear an oven mitt when removing a hot bowl from the microwave.

HOW TO SAFELY STORE YOUR PRODUCTS

It's best to use glass containers, not plastic, to store any recipe that contains essential oils, because the essential oils can deteriorate plastic over time. All of the recipes in this book make small batches since they are natural and don't contain preservatives.

Unless indicated otherwise, the finished products should be stored in a cool, dry place and should be used within two to four weeks. Never use a recipe if it looks like it has grown mold, if it has changed colors, or if it begins to smell bad.

ALLERGIES

Some people have skin sensitivities and allergies. Check with your doctor or dermatologist before using any of these recipes.

CLEAN UP

Many of the recipes in this book use oils and butters, which might feel greasy. To clean up, wipe your hands and any used dishes with a dry paper towel first, then use soap and water to wash. When using recipes in the bathtub, such as sugar scrubs, wipe the floor clean with a dry towel afterward. Oils and butters can make surfaces slippery and unsafe.

WHERE TO FIND PACKAGING FOR YOUR PRODUCTS

It's important to use brand new containers to store your products. It will help prevent mold from growing. Here's where you can buy containers that are perfect for the recipes in this book:

• reusable 2-ounce (59-milliliter) glass bottles or 4-ounce (118-mL) glass containers can be found in the essential oil aisle at health food stores

• reusable 2-ounce (59-mL) plastic spray bottles or 3-ounce (89-mL) plastic squeeze bottles can be found in the travel section of grocery or convenience stores

• reusable 4-ounce (118-mL) spice tins or empty spice jars can be found in the bulk spice aisle in grocery stores or health food stores

• half-pint glass jars can be found in the jam or canning aisle in grocery stores or health food stores

• round plastic containers with screw-top lids can be found in the jewelry or bead storage aisle at craft stores or in the travel aisle of department stores

Creaseless Hair Tie

You will need:

fold-over elastic (½ inch or 1.2 centimeter in width)
clear nail polish
scissors

It's super easy to make your own fancy hair ties. All you need is fold-over elastic, which is a soft, stretchy ribbon that can be found in the sewing aisle of craft stores. It comes in lots of fun colors and patterns.

DIRECTIONS:

Cut a 10-inch (25-cm) long piece of fold-over elastic. Fold it in half lengthwise, then tie the ends together into a knot. Pull tightly to secure. Line the raw edges with a thin line of clear nail polish to prevent fraying. Let dry overnight.

Ribbon Headband

You will need:

hair band
3 colors of ribbon
cloth measuring tape
scissors

These colorful stretchy headbands are addicting to make. You might have to make one for each of your friends! Once you get the hang of it, get creative with your materials. Try braiding together textured ribbon, fabric scraps, or leather cord. What else can you dream up?

DIRECTIONS:

With a cloth measuring tape, measure around your head as if you were wearing an elastic headband. Add 6 inches (15 cm) to that measurement. Now cut three ribbons to that length. Knot one end to a hair band by stacking the three ribbons, then threading the ends through the center of the hair band and back around to form a loop. Push the ends of the ribbon through the loop and pull tightly.

Hook the hair band onto a doorknob or cabinet knob and begin braiding the ribbon. When about 3 inches (7.5 cm) remain, knot the remaining ribbon onto the hair band following the same directions above. Pull tightly and trim ends.

Spa Hair Wrap

You will need:

30 x 54 inch (76 x 137 cm) bath towel,
or two 16 x 28 inch (40.5 x 71 cm)
hand towels

fold-over elastic (½ inch or
1.2 cm in width)

fabric glue

scissors

Have you ever wrapped your hair up in a towel only to have the towel fall off your head? This craft turns a towel (a thin one works best) into a perfectly-sized wrap that will help your hair dry quickly.

Tip: Pick out a towel with a bold color or pattern, or add your own designs with a fabric marker.

DIRECTIONS:

If using a bath towel, fold it in half lengthwise. If using two hand towels, stack them on top of each other. Draw the shape shown in the bottom left image on your towel with a fabric marker. Use the finished seam as the bottom of the pattern. It should measure 25 inches (63.5 cm) long and be 10 inches (25.5 cm) high at its highest point. Cut out pattern when done.

Remove top layer and set aside. Cut a 4-inch (10-cm) piece of fold-over elastic and fold it in half. Glue the ends together so it forms a loop. Then glue the loop to the left edge of your towel, about four inches (10 cm) from the bottom seam.

On the bottom layer of fabric, glue a line about ½ inch (1.2 cm) in from the edge, leaving the finished bottom edge unglued. Place the second layer of towel on top and press firmly along the glued edges. Let dry overnight. When dry, turn the towel inside out.

Deep Conditioning Treatment

Give your hair the ultimate conditioning treatment. The oils and butters in this recipe can work wonders on dry hair. To use, massage a very small amount into damp hair. Leave on for 10 minutes, then shampoo and condition as usual. This balm can also be used sparingly as a leave-in conditioner on the ends of dry hair. Massage mixture into your hands first, then rub hands along ends of hair.

DIRECTIONS:

Scoop shea butter into a microwave-safe bowl with a pourable spout. Microwave in 30-second increments at 50 percent power, stirring each time, until it mostly liquefies. Remove bowl with oven mitt. Stir in coconut oil until mixture is clear, not cloudy. Add jojoba oil and stir. Pour into a jar. Let sit overnight so oils and butter can cool to form a cream.

Dry Shampoo

Greasy hair? No problem! Dry shampoo can give your hair a pick-me-up when you don't have time to wash it. Use a spice jar so you can easily sprinkle this powder onto your hair, or dip a makeup brush in a jar and brush the powder onto your hair. Apply the powder sparingly to greasy sections of hair.

cornstarch

For light hair

You will need:

¼ cup (60 mL) cornstarch
1 tbsp (15 mL) baking soda
2 drops lavender essential oil
(optional)

For dark hair

You will need:

2 tbsp (30 mL) cornstarch
2 tbsp (30 mL) unsweetened
cocoa powder
1 tsp (5 mL) baking soda
2 drops peppermint essential oil
(optional)

DIRECTIONS:

Combine all ingredients in a bowl and stir. Scoop into container
and store in a cool, dry place.

Surf Spray

You will need:

3 tbsp (45 mL) aloe vera gel
1 tbsp (15 mL) distilled water
2 tsp (10 mL) fine sea salt

Get beachy waves with this salt spray gel. To use, spray lightly onto slightly damp hair, then scrunch your locks! The salt in the spray can help form soft waves that will make you look like you just got back from a dip in the ocean.

sea salt

Be careful! Sea salt sprays can damage hair if used too often, because salt has a drying effect. Be sure to condition your hair after using this spray.

DIRECTIONS:

Mix ingredients in a bowl with a pourable spout. Pour into a 2-ounce (59-mL) spray bottle.

Tame Those Tangles Spray

You will need:

3 tbsp (45 mL) apple cider vinegar
3 tbsp (45 mL) distilled water
15 drops lavender essential oil
   (optional)

Here's a recipe that will not only tame your tangles, but also leave your hair with a nice shine. The lavender essential oil will help mask the strong smell of vinegar. To use, apply to damp hair (focusing on tangles), then brush through hair. Shake before each use.

DIRECTIONS:

Mix all ingredients in glass bowl with pourable spout.
Pour into a 2-ounce (59-mL) reusable spray bottle.

Hair Spray

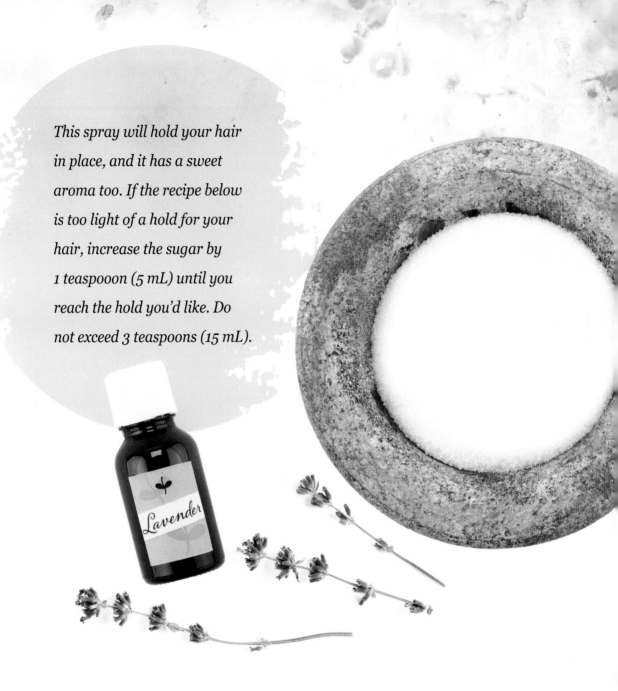

This spray will hold your hair in place, and it has a sweet aroma too. If the recipe below is too light of a hold for your hair, increase the sugar by 1 teaspooon (5 mL) until you reach the hold you'd like. Do not exceed 3 teaspoons (15 mL).

Lavender

DIRECTIONS:

Lightly boil water. Stir in sugar until water is clear, not cloudy. Remove from heat and let cool. Pour into glass bowl with pourable spout. Add essential oil and stir. Makes enough for two 2-ounce (59-mL) spray bottles.

Hair Perfume Spray

You will need:

- 5 tbsp (75 mL) rosewater
- 1 tbsp (15 mL) aloe vera gel
- 5 drops Roman chamomile essential oil
- 2 drops orange essential oil
- 5 drops lavender essential oil

We love this recipe because it makes your hair smell like a summer breeze, and it also acts as a nourishing leave-in conditioner. Spray on wet hair right after the shower or spray onto dry hair that needs a bit of a pick-me-up. Shake before each use.

Be careful! Close your eyes when using this spray.

DIRECTIONS:

Mix all ingredients in a bowl with a pourable spout.
Pour into a 2-ounce (59-mL) spray bottle.

Beautiful Hair Clips

Give your boring bobby pins a makeover! This simple craft takes just a few minutes and uses nail polish as decorative paint. These pins can be customized for any holiday or season, and they make great gifts too.

DIRECTIONS:

Stack parchment paper on top of cardboard. Then slip the bobby pins onto the stacked cardboard and paper. Make sure the bobby pins are spaced out evenly. Lay a second sheet of parchment paper under the cardboard to protect your surface. Paint each bobby pin with a layer of nail polish. Let dry, then add a second layer. Use a toothpick to add polka dots or stripes. Let dry overnight, then remove the pins from cardboard.

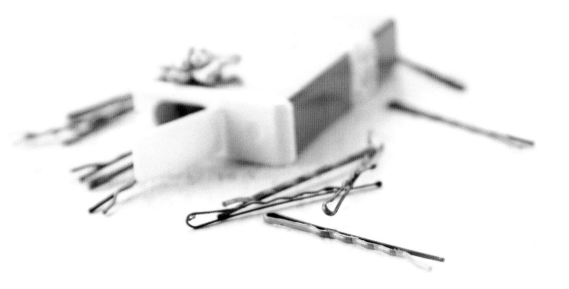

Hair Clip Case

You can never have enough bobby pins, right? They always seem to disappear. But now that your bobby pins are no longer boring, you won't want to lose them. Keep them organized in this cute case.

You will need:

empty plastic candy case, like Tic Tac
nail polish
parchment paper
ribbon (optional)
stickers (optional)

DIRECTIONS:

Protect your surface with a sheet of parchment paper. Now begin painting your plastic case with nail polish. Try polka dots, stripes, or paint splatters. Let dry overnight, then fill it with your beautiful bobby pins! Finish the case with ribbon or stickers, if you'd like.

Glam Twisted Headband

Turn an old pair of tights into a super cute hair wrap with a fashionable knot in front. The stretch in the tights and the stretch of a hair band ensure this wrap fits snugly around your head.

DIRECTIONS:

Cut the leg portions off of a pair of tights. Lay one leg horizontally and the next leg vertically on top of it to form a cross. Fold over the left side to the right side and the top to the bottom. Grab the ends of each side and pull until the lengths are even. Thread each end of the tights through the center of the hair band and knot the ends around the band. Trim any excess material.

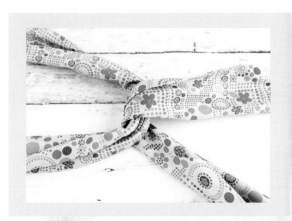

Hair Masks

With one of these nourishing hair masks, your locks will soon look and feel lovelier than ever! To use, apply evenly to your hair, then place a shower cap (or plastic wrap) over your hair. Leave the mask on for 10 minutes, then rinse it out in the shower. Shampoo and condition as usual.

No More Frizz Mask

Strengthen your hair and reduce frizz at the same time with this nourishing mask.

You will need:

1 ripe banana
¼ cup (60 mL) plain yogurt, or more for longer hair
1 tbsp (15 mL) honey

DIRECTIONS:

Put banana and yogurt in a bowl and mix and mash together with a fork. Add honey and stir until blended well. Makes 1 mask.

Itchy Scalp Mask

If your scalp is feeling dry and you're fighting dandruff, give this moisturizing mask a try.

You will need:

½ ripe avocado
¼ cup (60 mL) mayonnaise, or more for longer hair
1 tbsp (15 mL) olive oil

DIRECTIONS:

Put avocado and mayonnaise in a bowl and mix and mash together with a fork. Add olive oil and stir until blended well. Makes 1 mask.

Smoothing Spray

You will need:

2 tbsp (30 mL) aloe vera gel
2 tbsp (30 mL) distilled water
1 tsp (5 mL) vegetable glycerin

Got frizz? Get rid of it! The aloe vera gel and glycerin in this recipe can help tame unruly manes. A few spritzes of this spray go a long way. Spray lightly on dry hair, then brush through. Shake before each use.

aloe vera gel

DIRECTIONS:

Mix all ingredients in a bowl with a pourable spout. Pour into a 2-ounce (59-mL) spray bottle.

Boho Hair Wrap

You will need:
embroidery floss
scissors

Give your hair a burst of temporary color with embroidery floss. You can even add charms, feathers, or beads if you dare! These wraps can be washed as usual in the shower but should be removed after two weeks. Or make your hair wrap removable by knotting the center of the embroidery floss to the end of a bobby pin (instead of the top of a braided piece of hair). Then follow the directions in the second paragraph below.

Tip: Try crisscrossing colors, looping the floss to create a friendship bracelet effect, or leave segments of your braid showing. Make an ombre effect by picking three shades of one color, then wrapping from light to dark or dark to light.

DIRECTIONS:

First, braid the piece of hair you'd like to wrap. Place a bobby pin at the end to temporarily secure it. Cut three colors of embroidery floss three times the length of your braid and gather them together. Tie the center of the embroidery floss in a tight knot at the top of the braid. Now six strings will hang loose.

Choose one piece of floss and start wrapping it around your hair, plus the other five pieces of floss. After about one inch, choose a different color floss and begin wrapping it around your hair and the other five pieces of floss. It doesn't have to be perfect. When you're done, tie the strings in a double knot.

Shimmer Hair Gel

A little shimmer never hurt anyone. Holiday colors and school spirit colors can make any hairdo extra festive. To use, dip fingers in jar and apply gel to hair. If this hold isn't strong enough for your hair, try making it with 1 teaspoon of gelatin.

DIRECTIONS:

Boil 1 cup (240 mL) of water. Add gelatin and stir until dissolved. Let cool. Using a funnel or a bowl with a pourable spout, pour into container. Let set in refrigerator overnight. Once gel has set, stir in glitter. Makes about 3 ounces (89 mL). This gel must be stored in the refrigerator when not in use.

Gift Idea: Hair Flair

The decorated hair clips (page 32) and the creaseless hair ties (page 14) are quick and easy gifts that everyone loves. Here's a super cute way to package these handmade crafts!

You will need:

jar
card stock
scissors
glitter
glue
colored marker

Glittery Hair Clip Carrier

Trace the bottom of a jar onto backside of card stock and cut along lines. Decorate the front side of card stock with glitter. Let glue dry before sliding decorated bobby pins onto the circle.

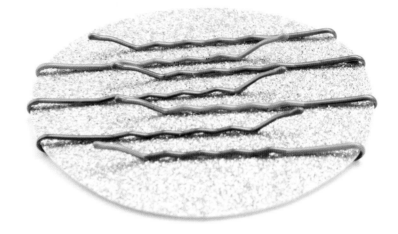

Hair Ties

Cut a 5 x 4 inch (13 x 10 cm) rectangle from plain card stock. Slide a few hair ties onto plain card stock. (If hair ties don't slide easily onto card stock, trim the card stock to be slimmer than 4 inches (10 cm) until hair ties fit.) If you want to add some flair, write a message with marker in between each hair tie.

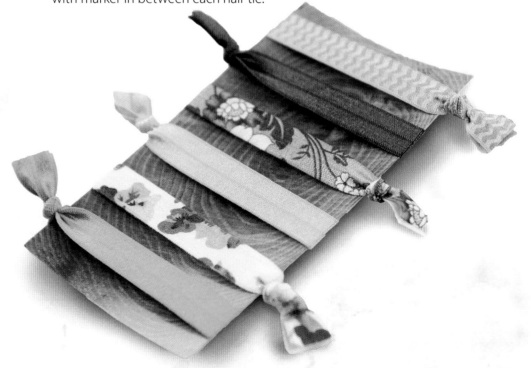

CONGRATS TO YOU!

You've made all-natural recipes that beautify your mind and body. Which one was your favorite? The calming or the rejuvenating? The scrubbing or the soothing?

It's important to pamper yourself every week—if not every day. Taking even just five minutes to relax with one of your favorite recipes can relieve stress, calm your nerves, and help you find focus.

Once you've spoiled yourself, don't forget to share the love by giving away these beauty products as gifts. Or throw a party and pamper your guests with spa-like treatments.

It's all about feeling beautiful in the skin you're in. When you feel beautiful, you look beautiful!

READ MORE

Beaumont, Mary Richards. *The Hair Book: Care & Keeping Advice for Girls*. Middleton, Wis.: American Girl, 2016.

Kenney, Karen Latchana. *Hair Care Tips & Tricks*. Style Secrets. Minneapolis: Lerner Publications, 2016.

Strebe, Jenny. *Braids & Buns, Ponies & Pigtails: 50 Hairstyles Every Girl Will Love*. San Francisco: Chronicle Books, 2016.

Titles in this set:

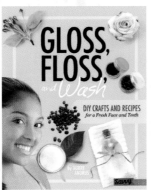

ABOUT THE AUTHOR

Aubre Andrus is an award-winning children's
book author with books published by Scholastic,
American Girl, and more. She cherishes her
time spent as the Lifestyle Editor of *American
Girl* magazine where she developed crafts,
recipes, and party ideas for girls. When she's not
writing, Aubre loves traveling around the world,
and some of her favorite places include India,
Cambodia, and Japan. She currently lives in
Los Angeles with her husband. You can find her
website at www.aubreandrus.com.